PIONEERS OF SCIENCE

EDWARD JENNER

Stephen Morris

The Bookwright Press
New York · 1992

Pioneers of Science

Archimedes
Alexander Graham Bell
Karl Benz
Marie Curie
Thomas Edison
Albert Einstein
Michael Faraday

Galileo
Edward Jenner
Joseph Lister
Guglielmo Marconi
Isaac Newton
Louis Pasteur
Leonardo da Vinci

First published in the
United States in 1992 by
The Bookwright Press
387 Park Avenue South
New York, NY 10016

First published in 1991 by
Wayland (Publishers) Ltd
61 Western Road, Hove
East Sussex BN3 1JD, England

Library of Congress Cataloging-in-Publication Data

Morris, Stephen.
  Edward Jenner/by Stephen Morris,
    p. cm. — (Pioneers of science)
  Includes index
  Summary: A biograph of the British physician who discovered the
smallpox vaccine.
  ISBN 0–531–18460–9
  1. Jenner, Edward. 1749–1823–Juvenile literature.   2. Physicians–
England–Biography–Juvenile literature.   3. Smallpox–Preventive
literature.   [1. Jenner, Edward. 1749–1823.   2. Physicians.]
I. Title.   II. Series.
R489.J5M67   1992
614.5′21′092–dc20
[B]   91–22574
                                                      CIP
                                                       AC

Typeset by DP Press Ltd, Sevenoaks, Kent
Printed in Italy by Rotolito Lombarda S.p.A.

Contents

The Smallpox Scourge

Edward Jenner was born in the mid-eighteenth century, in Berkeley, a village in the center of England. The second half of the eighteenth century was a time of great change in England. The Industrial Revolution was under way: the mechanization of spinning cotton and wool, the use of steam power in industry and a program of canal building, for example, were all affecting the way people lived and worked. There was also a scientific revolution at this time, and there were many discoveries, such as that of nitrous oxide

Knights sailing to take part in the Crusades, in the Holy Land. The returning knights spread smallpox to European countries.

(laughing gas), later to be used as an anesthetic, and oxygen.

In spite of these advances, huge numbers of people were still falling victim to killer diseases. Today, we know the cause of most diseases, but in the eighteenth century many diseases were shrouded in mystery. The measures that were used in trying to control disease suggest that some diseases were regarded as contagious – capable of being passed from one person to another. Often, infected people would be kept apart or restricted as to where they could go.

Throughout history, one disease, smallpox, was feared the most. It killed a large proportion of the population, and those that survived were left with pockmarks (deep scars). King Louis XV of France (1710–74) was so badly pockmarked that the pitted scars made him look as if he had two noses!

The meeting of the Spanish conquistador (conqueror), Cortez, and the Aztec emperor of Mexico, Montezuma, in 1519. Smallpox was carried to North and South America by European settlers, where it killed millions of the native peoples.

Smallpox scars have been found on Egyptian mummies. The disease was endemic (widely present) in India and the Middle East and was spread to Europe in the thirteenth century by knights returning from the Crusades. Later the disease was spread to the Americas by the Spaniards and other settlers from Europe, where it devastated the native populations.

It had been known from early times that it would be very unlikely for anyone who survived smallpox to catch the disease again. In India and China, thousands of years ago, healthy people were given a mild attack of the disease so that they would be immune, or protected, from a bad

Portrait of King Louis XV of France. Like many other people of his time, he had his portrait painted without the pockmarks that spoiled his looks.

Lady Mary Wortley Montagu first saw smallpox inoculation in Turkey and felt it was her duty to spread the news of its benefits on her return to England in 1718.

infection. This is called variolation and, in those times, dried smallpox scabs were ground into powder and then blown through a tube into the nose of the patient.

Another method of variolation is inoculation, a word first used by Dr. Emanuel Timoni in 1714, to describe the method of introducing the matter from a smallpox pustule of a victim into the skin of a healthy person by the scratch of a needle. This method was used in Turkey, and Lady Mary Wortley Montagu, who had lived there for a while as wife to the British ambassador, played a leading role in promoting the benefits of inoculation in Britain starting in 1718.

Smallpox disease

The medical name for smallpox is variola, and it can pass from one person to another, by direct contact, by droplet infection (from coughs and sneezes), and by handling infected clothing or bedclothes.

Once the disease is inside the body, symptoms start after twelve to fourteen days, and include headache, fever, shivering and backache. After about three days, itching spots start to appear that may spread over the whole body. The spots then change to blisters that are at first watery (vesicles), but soon become pus filled (pustules, see below). The pustules then dry out and fall off, leaving deep scars. Anyone who survives the disease may also suffer from brain damage, deafness, pneumonia and nephritis, a painful kidney disease. Between a quarter and a half of those who caught a bad case of smallpox died. In the hundred years before Jenner was born, it is estimated that 60 million people in Europe died from the disease.

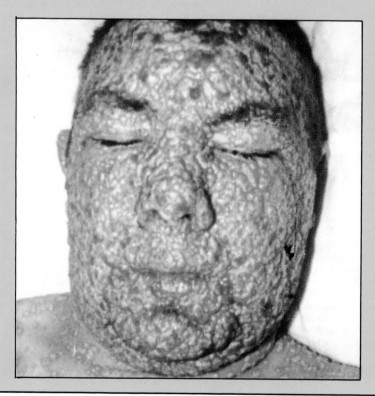

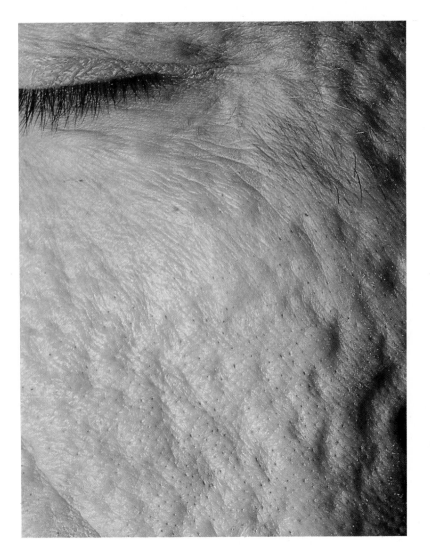

But inoculation did not stop smallpox from spreading. In fact, it had the opposite effect. Through inoculation, smallpox was introduced to areas where it was not endemic, so the technique itself was spreading the disease.

Despite the popularity of inoculation, some doctors believed there must be a better, less risky solution to the problem of making people immune to smallpox. There was an old "folk belief" that if someone had had an infection called cowpox – a disease caught from touching the infected teats and udders of cows – it would provide immunity against smallpox. But before Jenner, no one took this belief seriously.

Edward Jenner first became fascinated by smallpox during his apprenticeship to Daniel Ludlow, a country surgeon.

Edward Jenner was born on May 17, 1749. His parents, the Reverend and Mrs. Stephen Jenner, had ten children, and Edward was the youngest. His father was vicar of Berkeley and rector of nearby Rockhampton in Gloucestershire. (The local landowner, the Earl of Berkeley, and his family, played a key role in helping Jenner in his later career.) One of Edward's older brothers, Stephen, had been educated at Oxford University and had followed his father into the Church. In 1754, Edward's father died and his mother became a semi-invalid. The boy was only five years old when these tragic events happened, and he went to live with Stephen, who had succeeded his father as rector of Rockhampton.

Until the age of eight, Edward was taught by his brother. He then went to a nearby school and, at the age of eleven, to Cirencester Grammar School. His studies there included Latin and Greek – subjects he needed to learn if he wished to go to university like Stephen. However, Edward did not excel as a scholar and he preferred to spend his spare time collecting fossils and dormice nests.

Edward's interest in natural history was probably the reason why Stephen encouraged him to train as a country surgeon, and at the age

John Hunter's home in Windmill Street, London. Edward studied medicine at Hunter's school of anatomy for two years.

of thirteen he became apprenticed to Daniel Ludlow, a well-known surgeon in Chipping Sodbury. Edward assisted Ludlow during surgical operations, in the setting of broken bones, in making up and delivering medicines and in helping with the general running of the country practice.

During this time, Edward became fascinated by a disease that was seen all too often – smallpox. He himself had been inoculated with smallpox when he was eight years old, and it was an ordeal from which he was slow to recover. (He became very sensitive to sudden, sharp noises, which was to distress him greatly when he was older.) Edward made many notes on the development of the disease and drew pictures of the rash as it went through its various stages. He also learned about cowpox and the way its rash developed.

At the age of twenty-one, Edward was persuaded to study medicine under the guidance of the great surgeon-anatomist John Hunter, who ran a school of anatomy in London. The two years of instruction were enjoyable for Edward, and he struck up a close friendship with Hunter. The two men remained good friends and corresponded regularly until Hunter's death in 1793.

Hunter collected animal and human specimens. Some were very unusual, such as this chicken.

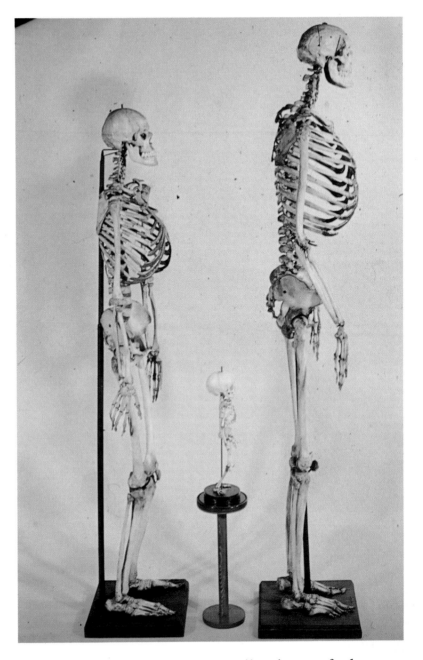

Hunter had a fine collection of human anatomical specimens (preserved examples of the human body) which fascinated Edward. One of Hunter's most famous items was the skeleton of an Irish giant, which can still be seen in the museum of the Royal College of Surgeons in London. Hunter also liked to study animals and compare their anatomy with that of humans. His menagerie was the forerunner of the London Zoo.

The English navigator and explorer Captain James Cook. He asked Edward if he would like to be his ship's naturalist, but Edward preferred to complete his studies and became a country surgeon.

In 1771, when Captain James Cook returned from the first of his explorations of the South Seas, Hunter recommended that Edward should work on preserving and cataloging some of the rare specimens that had been brought back for exhibition. This was a great compliment for the young man, who performed the task with enthusiasm. Captain Cook was greatly impressed by his work and asked if Edward would come with him on the next expedition as the ship's naturalist. This was a wonderful opportunity, but Edward did not take it up. Instead, he completed his studies and earned the certificates he needed to be a country surgeon, and in 1772 he returned to Berkeley to set up in medical practice.

The Country Surgeon

Jenner was a popular figure in Berkeley. He treated all his patients with care and devotion and, sometimes, his friends enjoyed traveling with him on his rounds to his patients in the surrounding farms and villages. We have an account of what he actually looked like through the writings of his closest friend, Edward Gardner. Gardner described Jenner as a man "small but of sturdy build, always smartly dressed in immaculate buckskin breeches, a blue coat with yellow buttons, shining riding boots with silver spurs and a broad-brimmed hat. His hair was cut short in a fashionable style of the time, called a cob."

John Hunter, the great surgeon-anatomist, who did so much to encourage Jenner to research into medical topics and natural history.

Jenner assisted in forming a medical society, which met at the Fleece Inn at the nearby village of Rodborough. Later he joined a medical club, which met at the Ship Inn at Alveston near Bristol. However, not all of the members were sympathetic to Jenner's ideas. Having returned to his study of cowpox and smallpox, he often voiced his opinion that there might be something in the folk belief that cowpox gave protection against smallpox. Some of his medical colleagues were skeptical and, fed up with the subject, tried to ban him from the medical clubs.

Jenner believed that there might be some truth in the folk belief that cowpox provided immunity to smallpox, and he made a detailed study of the two diseases.

As a country surgeon, Jenner often treated milkmaids for the disease, cowpox. Milkmaids were often noted for their unpockmarked faces, which became the subject of a popular rhyme.

Jenner's opinion can be traced back to the time when he was an apprentice to Daniel Ludlow. A dairymaid came to be treated for an infected hand, and she described in detail how the rash developed. He was struck by her remark that she could not have smallpox because she had had cowpox. At that time there was a popular rhyme:

> "Where are you going to my pretty maid?"
> "I'm going a milking, sir," she said.
> "What is your fortune my pretty maid?"
> "My face is my fortune, sir," she said.

The unpockmarked faces of the milkmaids were such a remarkable sight in those days that Jenner was convinced there must be a connection between the diseases. But how could he prove this? He must have discussed the matter on many occasions with Ludlow and with Hunter.

Viruses – a cause of disease

Smallpox is caused by a virus (below), a living organism that is too small to be seen with an ordinary microscope – a powerful electron microscope is needed. The virus survives by entering a living cell where it reproduces itself. Viruses cause many diseases including the common cold, influenza, measles, mumps, chickenpox, polio, rabies and AIDS.

The word "virus" was used in Elizabethan times, when it meant a venom or a poisonous substance. Jenner was one of the first people to use the word to describe a disease, and since his time it has been adopted as a medical term.

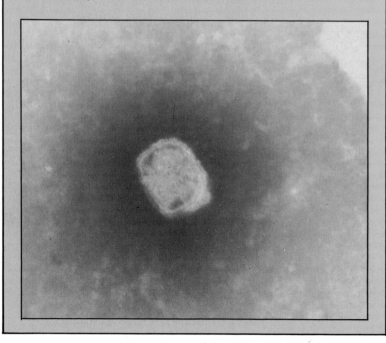

Jenner realized that the first step would be to define exactly what was true cowpox and what was smallpox – in the early stages the two diseases looked very much alike. In addition to his detailed notes, he made drawings of the different rashes and pustules. It was slow and sometimes frustrating work, and not helped by those who criticized his ideas.

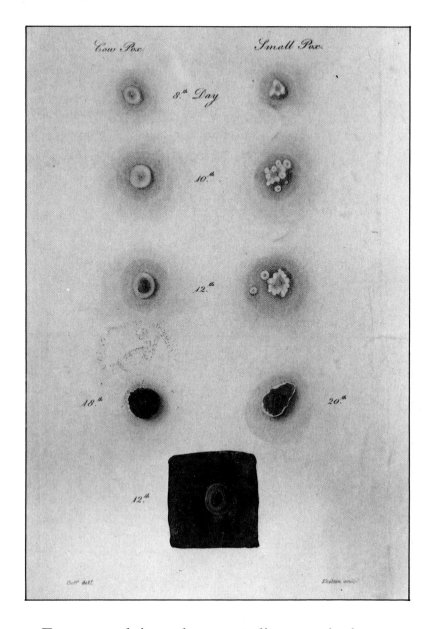

Jenner's drawings of the differences between cowpox pustules (left) and smallpox pustules. The two pustules on the "8th Day" show that during the early stages, the two diseases were very similar.

From studying the two diseases it became apparent to Jenner that milkmaids often suffered from several different kinds of skin infections, and not just cowpox. He became interested in a rash of the skin found on the heels of horses, called "grease." There was some evidence that this, or a form of it, could be passed to cows and from them to milkmaids. This must have complicated the picture, but Jenner persevered with his work, gathering together as much evidence as he could on the subject.

4 The Medical Scientist and Naturalist

Berkeley was noted for its extremes in weather conditions. The winters could be severe, and the first recorded account of a case of hypothermia was that of Jenner himself. Hypothermia is a dangerous condition in which a person's temperature drops below normal, 98.6°F (37°C). If hypothermia is prolonged, it can be fatal. Jenner was visiting a patient during a blizzard in January 1786 when, as he later recorded, "As the sense of external cold increased, the heat about the stomach seemed to increase . . . My hands at last grew extremely painful, and this distressed my spirits . . . when I came to the house I was unable to dismount without assistance. I was almost senseless . . . The parts which had been most benumbed, felt for some time as if they had been slightly burned."

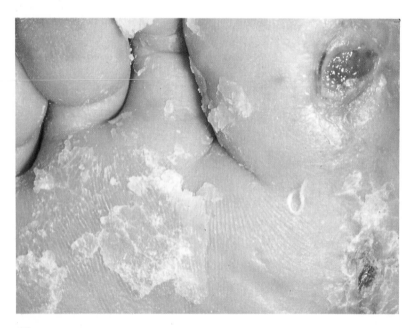

Frostbitten toes. Frostbite is caused by the freezing of body tissues, and it commonly affects the fingers, ears, toes, and nose. Almost certainly, Jenner would have developed a bad case of frostbite if he had not warmed himself slowly after his journey in the blizzard in 1786.

Despite his condition, he had the presence of mind to prevent those who came to his assistance from sitting him in front of the fire. Instead, he stayed in the stable for some time and rubbed his hands in the snow to relieve the pain. Today, doctors know that people suffering from hypothermia should not be warmed up rapidly; in extreme cases frostbite occurs and causes the tissues in the affected part to die or decay. This is called gangrene and can be fatal if the affected part is not removed.

Climbers and other people exposed to the elements have to protect themselves from the dangers of hypothermia. In cold weather, old people may suffer from loss of body heat. Jenner's account of the effects of hypothermia was the first to be recorded.

Jenner was also interested in the heart and how the blood circulates around the body. While studying in London, he and John Hunter had noticed that the arteries of people who were known to have died suddenly, following severe chest pain, were often hard and narrow and blocked by clotted blood. He wrote to a noted physician of the day, Dr. William Heberden, to tell him of their findings – Dr. Heberden had named the chest pain prior to death "angina pectoris." In 1777, Hunter himself began to suffer from chest pains, and this caused anxiety to Jenner. In fact, Hunter lived another sixteen years – he finally collapsed and died during a heated debate with some students on October 16, 1793.

Jenner did not spend all his time studying medical problems. Despite the heavy workload as a country surgeon, he had many different interests and hobbies. His love of the countryside was expressed in poetry. One poem, *Berkeley Fair*, which became quite famous, was about the annual May Fair where he lived.

A letter from Hunter suggesting that Jenner should try "the experiment on a hedgehog."

Jenner discovered that when a hedgehog's temperature dropped to below 30°F (−1°C) it became sleepy. During the cold winter months, hedgehogs remain inactive, or dormant.

Between 1775 and 1786, Jenner carried out research into natural history, not only for his own benefit but also to assist Hunter in his research and to help build up his collection of natural history specimens. Both men had long been interested in the subject of body temperature and how it changed while animals hibernated. Hunter was particularly interested in the behavior of the hedgehog, and he asked Jenner to send him specimens, since hedgehogs were hard to find in London. Jenner also carried out some experiments on Hunter's behalf. He discovered that if a hedgehog's temperature dropped below 30°F (−1°C), which is below freezing point, it became sleepy and showed no desire to eat. But when the temperature of the creature rose to 93°F (34°C) it immediately became hungry.

Jenner helped Hunter in other investigations. He had told Hunter about unusual calves that had both male and female sex organs, and Hunter later presented the findings to the members of the Royal Society in London. Besides hedgehogs, Jenner sent Hunter bats, eels, fossils and, on one occasion, a small whale that had been washed up on the banks of the nearby Severn River.

Ornithology, the study of birds, was a particular interest of Jenner's. Hunter encouraged him to study the cuckoo and, in the winter of 1786–7, he wrote a paper (a report of his work) entitled *The Natural History of the Cuckoo*. The paper contained several new observations about the bird, some of which were met with disbelief when it was read to the Royal Society in March 1787. Despite this, Jenner's contribution to the understanding of the natural world was

A newly hatched cuckoo pushes out an egg from a reed warbler's nest. Jenner studied the cuckoo, and he discovered that it could push out an egg only in the first few days of its life.

recognized on February 26, 1789, when he was elected Fellow of the Royal Society – a great honor for any man of science.

Later, Jenner was to study the migration of birds. At the time, many people thought that birds that were seen only in the summer either hibernated or spent time submerged in water or mud. Jenner proved that neither of these explanations was true. He also made the observation that migrating birds tended to return each year to their previous nests, and once they had produced their offspring they were ready to fly south again.

Jenner's work as a naturalist is often overshadowed by the recognition and fame he earned for his work producing a vaccine for smallpox, but it is all part of the background from which vaccination came.

A swallow feeding its young. Jenner proved that migrating birds, such as the swallow, were ready to fly south once their young could fend for themselves.

5 Vaccination Experiments

The small, thatched building in the grounds of Jenner's Berkeley home, where he studied cowpox and smallpox. It is sometimes referred to as the "Temple of Vaccinia."

During the time Jenner was studying the cuckoo, he met and fell in love with a young woman named Catherine Kingscote, and they were married on March 6, 1788. Jenner and his bride moved into a house in Berkeley – until then he had been living with his brother Stephen. Their marriage was very happy, and in 1789 their first son, Edward, was born. Later they had a second son, Robert, and a daughter, Catherine. In the grounds of the Jenner's home was a small thatched building with a single room. It was here that Jenner was to continue his work on cowpox and smallpox. He knew that he had studied the two diseases long enough – now was the time to put his ideas into action and to try vaccination: to inoculate a person with a preparation of cowpox to see if it produced immunity to smallpox.

In his first experiment he vaccinated his baby, Edward, not with cowpox, but with swinepox, to see if this would give protection against smallpox. It may have worked; at any rate, the child grew up without catching the dreaded disease. He gave his son swinepox because there was no cowpox in the area at the time.

Jenner's work was tiring and, in 1794, he caught the disease typhus, which gave him a fever, severe headaches and a skin rash. When he recovered, he returned to his experiments, recording twelve people who had had cowpox in earlier life who, when inoculated with smallpox, experienced no reaction. He also found three cases of people who had developed immunity to smallpox after suffering from the horse disease, grease.

Jenner's drawing of cowpox pustules on the hand of the dairymaid Sarah Nelmes.

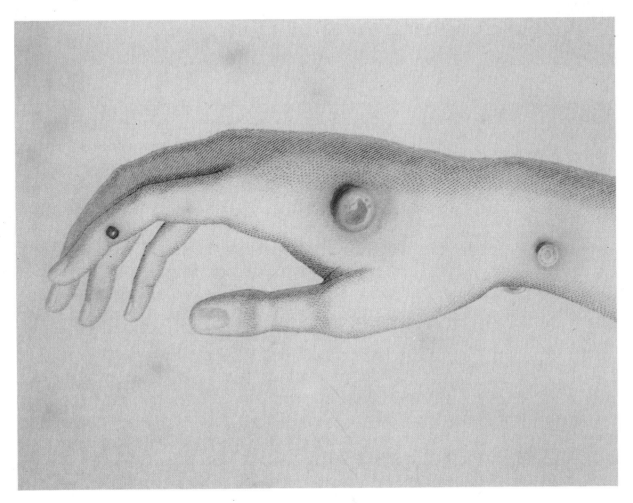

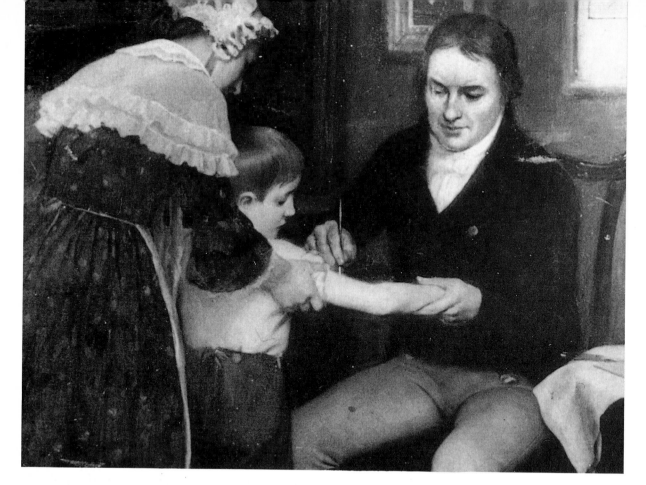

Jenner inoculates James Phipps with smallpox after the boy had been given cowpox. James did not suffer from smallpox and lived to enjoy his old age.

On May 14, 1796, Jenner had the opportunity to put his theory to the ultimate test – to inoculate a person with cowpox and then give them smallpox to see if there was any effect. A dairymaid named Sarah Nelmes, who had "contracted cowpox from her master's cows," was seen by Jenner. She had a large sore on her hand from which he took some fluid and injected it into the arm of a healthy eight-year-old boy named James Phipps. In a short time, James developed cowpox, becoming restless and suffering from headaches. But by May 24, Jenner reported "he was perfectly well." Then, on July 1, Jenner inoculated James with smallpox, which produced no effect. Naturally, Jenner was thrilled by the outcome, and on July 19 he wrote to his friend Edward Gardner, telling him of the historic event saying, "I shall now pursue my experiments with redoubled ardor."

Solving the mystery of disease

The cause of infectious diseases was a mystery until the end of the nineteenth century. Small organisms had been observed by a Dutchman, Antoni Leeuwenhoek (1632–1723), under his simple microscope. But the significance of this discovery was not fully appreciated until a Frenchman, Louis Pasteur (1822–95), clearly established a theory that infectious diseases were caused by minute organisms. Most of the experiments carried out by Pasteur were with organisms called bacteria which, unlike viruses, could be seen under a microscope and, therefore, identified.

Proof that viruses existed came in 1898, when it was shown that a highly infectious disease of cattle, pigs, sheep and goats, called foot-and-mouth disease, could be transmitted by bacteria-free infectious material. Once it was known there were organisms that were ultra-small but yet infectious, work could begin on identifying the causes of many comon diseases, and vaccines could be developed to combat them.

The body's natural defenses

The body's immune system is designed to combat the infections that will kill or do harm, if left unchecked. Fortunately, the majority of the infections in healthy people do not last long and leave little permanent damage. The immune system makes use of two forms of defense. One is a rapid form that has no "memory" of the encounter with the invading organism. The second has a "memory system," so if the same organism is encountered again, a rapid and effective defense is put into action. Vaccination is aimed at this second defense system. Immunity to certain diseases is not always long-lasting. This is why revaccination or "booster" doses of vaccine are sometimes given.

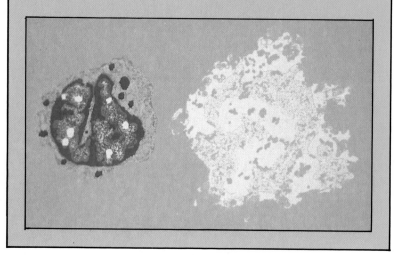

One of the body's "killer" cells (left) after it has attacked an invading organism. Killer cells like this are part of the body's immune system, which protects us against diseases.

The experiment had proved successful, but Jenner knew that many more experiments would be required to prove his theory conclusively. Unfortunately for Jenner, cases of cowpox were not always available, and he had to wait for two years before he could carry out a series of vaccination experiments. Three men on a farm caught cowpox in April 1798, and Jenner seized his chance. He inoculated several children and adults with cowpox, and all of them later resisted the smallpox infection.

AN

INQUIRY

INTO

THE CAUSES AND EFFECTS

OF

THE VARIOLÆ VACCINÆ,

A DISEASE

DISCOVERED IN SOME OF THE WESTERN COUNTIES OF ENGLAND,

PARTICULARLY

GLOUCESTERSHIRE,

AND KNOWN BY THE NAME OF

THE COW POX.

BY EDWARD JENNER, M.D. F.R.S. &c.

———— QUID NOBIS CERTIUS IPSIS
SENSIBUS ESSE POTEST, QUO VERA AC FALSA NOTEMUS.

LUCRETIUS.

London:

PRINTED, FOR THE AUTHOR,

BY SAMPSON LOW, N°. 7, BERWICK STREET, SOHO:

AND SOLD BY LAW, AVE-MARIA LANE; AND MURRAY AND HIGHLEY, FLEET STREET.

1798.

Soon after this, he wrote the first summary of his observations which was titled *On the Cowpox, the Original Paper*, but it was not printed. Then in June 1798, he published a fuller account: *An Inquiry into the Causes and Effects of the Variolae Vaccinae, a Disease Discovered in some of the Western Counties of England, Particularly Gloucestershire, and Known by the Name of the Cowpox*. It comprised seventy-five pages and included a drawing of the hand of Sarah Nelmes among the colored pictures of cowpox and smallpox. Jenner updated the *Inquiry* in 1799 and 1800. It was translated into several languages and was often reprinted – particularly during outbreaks of smallpox in the nineteenth century.

6 Spreading the Message of Vaccination

Immediately before the *Inquiry* was printed, Jenner traveled to London, hoping to demonstrate his method to those who were interested. But no one was. After three months of disappointment, he returned to Berkeley, but before leaving London he gave some of his dried cowpox lymph to a surgeon, Henry Cline, at St. Thomas's Hospital.

Opposite *A nineteenth-century picture of Jenner inoculating a child with cowpox.*

Left *The Compte de Mirabeau, the French revolutionary politician (1749–91). The most obvious effect of smallpox is scarring, but it can also cause deafness, pneumonia or brain damage.*

Cline was not very interested in the cowpox theory, but he did decide to make use of the lymph in an experiment on a patient of his, a boy with a diseased hip. The hip was giving the boy a lot of pain, and Cline was going to try a method of treatment, called counter-irritation, which involved applying an irritant to the skin in order to take away some of the pain. He inoculated the boy's hip with the cowpox lymph and in a day or two he developed the disease. It is not known if the counter-irritation treatment worked, but Cline then decided to test Jenner's claim and, accordingly, he inoculated the boy with smallpox. A Dr. Lister, who specialized in treating smallpox, witnessed Cline's experiment. Both men were pleased and surprised to find that the boy did not develop smallpox.

Jenner had to put up with some opposition to his ideas. This cartoon makes fun of his work. The caption to it reads: "The cow pock … or … the wonderful effects of the new inoculation!"

The Cow Pock — or — the Wonderful Effects of the New Inoculation! Vide the Publications of ý Anti Vaccine Society.

In a letter to Jenner, Cline wrote, "I think the substituting of cowpox poison for the smallpox promises to be one of the greatest improvements that there has ever been made in medicine . . ." After this, the cowpox theory became the talk of London's social and medical world. But Jenner still had to contend with some opposition, and with the general misunderstanding about the recognition of true cowpox and the method needed to vaccinate a person correctly.

One man, a Dr. Pearson, even tried to claim that he was the discoverer of the new cowpox vaccination procedure. With others, he formed a "Vaccine Board" and set up as a business to vaccinate paying customers. But Pearson could hardly tell cowpox from smallpox and, in one incident, all fourteen people he inoculated became gravely ill and one died. Pearson even invited Jenner to pay for the privilege of joining the Board, but Jenner refused to have anything to do with it.

Worried by the number of doctors who used the wrong lymph, Jenner thought of returning to London. Indeed, Cline wrote to him urging him to do so, assuring him that he would not have to worry about paying for a stay as he would have a large income from a vaccination practice. Jenner wrote in answer that, for the time being, he was content to remain in Gloucestershire.

A great part of his time was now spent in countering claims on his work and in sending cowpox lymph to vaccinators throughout Britain and to countries abroad where his work had become known. On January 31, 1800, Jenner came to London and met a supporter, Lord Egremont, to discuss the formation of a proper vaccine institution. In February, he traveled to Lord Egremont's estate in Sussex and successfully vaccinated nearly two hundred people.

Lord Egremont supported Jenner's work and was eager to establish a proper vaccination board.

In March, Jenner met King George III, and a month later, the commander-in-chief of the army invited him to vaccinate a whole regiment. In the following year, he was invited to vaccinate the sailors of the British fleet. The personal interest of the Royal Family in vaccination, and the importance the armed forces gave to it, did much to give Jenner's work the credit it deserved, for many people were ridiculing it. One doctor even claimed that people would come to look like animals if they were inoculated with cowpox!

Jenner's work as a country surgeon began to suffer and he found himself in financial difficulties. An increasing amount of his time was spent furthering the cause of vaccination, which meant traveling a great deal. The King understood his position and recommended that Jenner should receive a sum of money from the Treasury – the government department in charge of finances.

A painting showing scenes from Jenner's life. At the top is the vicarage where Jenner was born, and at the bottom is Berkeley church where he is buried.

After debating the worthiness of the recommendation, Parliament eventually approved an award.

Jenner returned to Berkeley and to his work as a country surgeon. He was supportive of a vaccination institution, the Royal Jennerian Institution, that had been formed "for the extermination of smallpox," and in February 1803 he traveled to London to busy himself with the institution's affairs. Unfortunately, when in London, he again found himself in financial difficulties and had to return to Gloucestershire and his work as a country surgeon. Then, in

An illustration showing French people (and a calf!) being inoculated against smallpox. In the nineteenth century, vaccination became compulsory in many countries.

1806, Parliament awarded Jenner £20,000, a considerable sum of money in those days.

By now, Jenner's name was becoming known worldwide. The Russian Emperor was so enthusiastic about vaccination that he ordered the vaccination of the entire population of the Russian Empire, and in 1812 it was reported that a total of 1,235,597 children had been vaccinated.

In 1801, Emperor Napoleon I of France sent a doctor to meet Jenner to learn all he could about vaccination in order to open a vaccine institute in Paris. Napoleon ordered the vaccination of the French troops, and in response to a letter from Jenner requesting the safe passage of two doctors at the time when France was at war with Britain, he is quoted to have said, "Jenner. Ah, we can refuse nothing to that man."

French soldiers being inoculated with cowpox. Emperor Napoleon Bonaparte was quick to realize the importance of Jenner's work and had his troops inoculated to improve their health and boost morale.

Gradually, reports of the effectiveness of vaccination became known. In 1802 vaccination began in Denmark, and in 1810 not a single case of smallpox was reported. In places as far apart as Germany and the Spanish colonies in South America, cases of smallpox became almost unknown after well-planned vaccination programs. In the United States, between 1801 and 1809, President Thomas Jefferson had all his family vaccinated and introduced vaccination to the native peoples of the United States. Before the Europeans arrived, smallpox had been unknown to the native tribes, but after its introduction, the disease caused the death of half the native American population. Vaccination relieved the suffering that smallpox caused, and in gratitude the Chiefs sent a letter to Jenner saying that "the Great Spirit" had been asked to "take care of him in this world and in the land of the spirits."

President Thomas Jefferson, who popularized vaccination in the United States.

7 The Defeat of Smallpox

With the reports of the effectiveness of vaccination came many honors and gifts for Jenner. He was congratulated personally by the Emperor of Russia and the King of Germany, and received a diamond ring and a pension from the Empress of Russia. In 1813, he received an honorary Doctorate of Medicine from Oxford University, which qualified him for membership of the Royal College of Physicians. However, the College insisted that he should take an examination in order to become a member. But Jenner, by now sixty-four years old, thought that at his age this was ridiculous and decided not to take the examination.

Just over forty years ago, the World Health Organization (WHO) identified smallpox as a disease that could be wiped out completely. The picture shows a vaccination team in Ethiopia. Market days were particularly busy for the team.

On September 14, 1815, Jenner's wife died of tuberculosis. They had been happily married for twenty-seven years, and Jenner never really recovered from the distress caused by her death. He continued to work as a medical scientist and naturalist, and during this time he wrote his paper on the migration of birds. In 1820 he suffered a slight stroke, but helped by the care of his daughter Catherine, he made a good recovery. In 1821, he was appointed Physician Extraordinary to King George IV and was also made Mayor of Berkeley and a Justice of the Peace.

On a bitterly cold morning in January 1823, Jenner walked to a nearby village to arrange for supplies of fuel to be delivered to some of his elderly patients. On his return home he suffered another stroke. He died two days later, on January 26, and was buried beside his wife in Berkeley church.

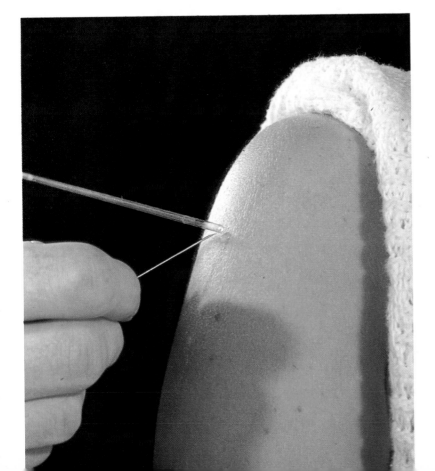

A person being given a smallpox vaccination. A two-pronged needle is used to prick the skin.

Jenner's work on smallpox and vaccination is seen as one of the great landmarks in the history of preventive medicine. In 1800, he had foreseen a time when the people of the world would no longer suffer from the terrible disease of smallpox, but it was not until recent times that anyone believed this would finally become possible.

There were several outbreaks of smallpox in Italy in 1853, in England in 1864, and in Australia and the United States in 1884, but that was because vaccination programs had become less strict. Vaccination subsequently became compulsory in many countries. In Britain, for example, several laws were passed after 1853, and remained in force until 1946, when compulsory vaccination was discontinued. But modern, fast methods of travel, especially by air, increased the risk of the spread of smallpox from countries where it remained endemic, to countries where it had been wiped out completely.

Two young children with smallpox. Thanks to the WHO campaign, scenes like this are no longer seen.

In 1949, the World Health Organization (WHO) identified smallpox as a disease that could be wiped out totally. A campaign was started, and by 1974 only four countries had cases of the disease. Slowly but surely, the last outbreaks of smallpox were treated – a difficult task in places where rugged terrain made it hard for medical teams to reach remote villages.

In May 1980, the WHO was able to report that the world was finally free of smallpox (the last recorded case was discovered on October 31, 1977). Supplies of the smallpox vaccine are still kept available in case there is an outbreak of the disease during a laboratory experiment with the virus.

The scroll declaring that smallpox had been wiped out totally from the world.

Modern vaccines

The words "vaccine" and "vaccinate" were first used by Jenner, and they come from the Latin word, *vacca*, which means "a cow." A hundred years ago, Louis Pasteur produced some solutions that gave immunity to several diseases. He used Jenner's word, vaccine, for these solutions. Pasteur laid the foundation of modern immunization, and many scientists since his time have worked to produce more effective and safer vaccines.

Many vaccines contain live bacteria or viruses that have been attenuated (weakened). Examples of attenuated organisms in vaccines are those used against the diseases measles, tuberculosis and rabies. Other vaccines consist of specially treated toxins – the poisonous substances that some organisms produce, causing severe illness. Examples of these vaccines are those used against diphtheria and tetanus. A third type of vaccine consists of dead organisms. Dead organisms are used against cholera and typhoid.

Despite the remarkable advances in immunization in the past one hundred years, many problems remain. For example, influenza can kill more people in eighteen months than were killed in battle during the World Wars I and II. Influenza is like smallpox in being one of the most lethal and impredictable of infections. The viruses that cause influenza frequently undergo a change, which means that scientists have to make a new vaccine for each "new" influenza virus.

This man, Ali Maow Maalin of Somalia, had the last recorded case of smallpox.

A laboratory technician prepares equipment used in the production of a vaccine, in this case against the disease hepatitis B. The work that Jenner pioneered two hundred years ago still continues today.

Doctors are still struggling to control some potentially lethal diseases. For example, influenza is a very unpredictable disease that has been compared with smallpox in the devastating effect it can have on large numbers of people. Another deadly disease, AIDS, is caused by the human immuno-deficiency virus (HIV). At present, doctors do not know how AIDS can be prevented, so the work that Jenner pioneered two hundred years ago still continues today.

Date Chart

1749 May 17: Edward Jenner born in Berkeley, Gloucestershire.

1754 Death of Jenner's parents. He goes to live with his brother Stephen.

1762 Apprenticed to Daniel Ludlow, a country surgeon in Chipping Sodbury.

1770 Becomes a pupil of John Hunter.

1772 Qualifies as surgeon and returns to Berkeley to set up his own practice.

1775 Studies hedgehog hibernation.

1786 Writes his observations on hypothermia.

1787 Paper on the cuckoo is read to the Royal Society.

1788 March 6: Jenner marries Catherine Kingscote.

1789 February 2: Elected Fellow of the Royal Society (FRS).

1793 John Hunter dies.

1796 May 14: vaccinates James Phipps with cowpox lymph from milkmaid Sarah Nelmes. Phipps is then inoculated with smallpox (July 1), but does not develop the disease.

1798 Publication of the *Inquiry* into cowpox. Travels to London to demonstrate his method but no one is interested.

1800 Successfully vaccinates an army regiment and nearly two hundred people on a Sussex estate.

1801 Vaccinates sailors of British fleet.

1802 Returns to Berkeley. Parliament awards a grant of £10,000.

1803 Helps in the running of the Royal Jennerian Institution.

1806 Parliament awards a further grant of £20,000.

1813 Receives an honorary Doctorate of Medicine from Oxford University.

1815 September 14: Catherine dies.

1820 Jenner suffers a mild stroke.

1821 Becomes Physician Extraordinary to King George IV; also becomes a Justice of the Peace.

1823 January 26: Jenner dies of a stroke.

1949 WHO identifies smallpox as a disease that can be eradicated.

1971 United States discontinues routine vaccination for smallpox.

1980 WHO announces the world is free of smallpox.

Books to Read

Balsamo, Kathey. *Exploring the Lives of Gifted People–The Sciences.* Carthage, IL: Good Apple, 1987.

Garrell, Dale C. and Solomon H. Snyder, eds. *Encyclopedia of Health.* New York: Chelsea House, 1988.

Young Scientist Book of Medicine Doctors and Health: How Illness Can Be Prevented and Cured. Tulsa, OK: EDC Publishing, 1986.

Glossary

Anatomist An expert in the physical structure of the body.

Anesthetic A gas or drug that causes a loss of sensation or pain. Anesthetics are used in surgical operations.

Bacteria Certain small organisms that can be seen under the microscope. Many types of bacteria cause disease.

Contagious Capable of being transmitted from one person to another.

Diseases Ailments caused by infections.

Electron microscope A powerful microscope that does not rely on light to produce a magnified image.

Endemic Occurring frequently in a particular region or population.

Folk belief An opinion held among country people that something is true, especially without proof.

Immune Protected against a particular infection.

Immunity The body's ability to resist infection.

Immunize To make a person immune by inoculation.

Infection Invasion of the body by harmful organisms.

Infectious Capable of being transmitted.

Inoculate To introduce a material into the body in order to induce immunity.

Lethal Causing death; deadly.

Lymph A fluid that flows through the body. Cowpox lymph was lymph taken from infected cows.

Menagerie A collection of animals.

Naturalist A person who is interested in animals and plants.

Organisms Living plants or animals.

Paper A formal essay on a subject.

Pockmarks Pitted scars left on the skin after pustules have healed.

Pustule A blister on the skin containing pus.

Scourge Something that causes suffering or destruction.

Specimen A whole or a part of an organism that has been preserved as an example of its type.

Stroke The name for an interruption of the flow of blood in the blood vessels of the brain or bleeding from those vessels.

Vaccination Originally a word used to describe inoculation with cowpox lymph, and used today for any injection employed to produce immunity to a particular disease.

Variolation The giving of a mild case of smallpox to a person in order to protect him or her from a bad infection of the disease.

Virus An ultra-small organism that can be seen only with an electron microscope. Viruses are the cause of many diseases.

Picture Acknowledgments

Bruce Coleman 23 (Andrew J. Purcell); Mary Evans iii, 6 (Explorer), 16, 17, 29, 32, 33, 34, 35, 37, 38, 39; J.E. Gethan-Jones 36; W.L. Gore & Associates 21; Eric and David Hosking 24, 25; The Jenner Museum, Berkeley 26; Mansell Collection 7; National Medical Slide Bank 8, 9; Royal College of Physicians 10; Reproduced with kind permission of the President and Council of the Royal College of Surgeons of England 10; Science Photo Library, 18, 20, 30, 41, 42, 45; Wayland Picture Library 4, 5, 14, 22, 31; WHO 28, 40, 43, 44.

Index